PLASTIC DONUTS

A FRESH
PERSPECTIVE
ON GIFTS

JEFF ANDERSON

Plastic Donuts

ISBN: 978-0-9848268-0-3

Printed in the United States of America

Endorsements

Jeff Anderson's insightful book gives us a fresh and well-constructed perspective on what it means to please God through our giving. Read it to gain refreshment for your soul and a challenge to grow more generous.

Chuck Bentley, CEO, Crown Financial Ministries

A Fresh Perspective on Gifts. That subtitle says it all. This is a very fresh work on the subject of stewardship for Christians. I welcome it as one of the best tools I've seen to put into the hands of any Christian who is serious about pleasing God in this important area of spiritual discipline. It gives you the sense of having plunged the depths of God's Word as it speaks to the matter of giving.

Pastor Hess Hester, Southern Hills Baptist Church

The plastic donut illustration immediately and emotionally drew me in, and helped me focus for the very first time on my Father's reaction to our giving. This understanding alone is transformational and worth so much. I especially like the "acceptable gift" perspective — This is needed.

Howard Dayton, Founder, Compass-finances God's way

This book is the next Treasure Principle. A paradigm shifting powerhouse.

Patrick Johnson - GenerousChurch, Chief Architect

In Plastic Donuts, Jeff provides a fresh and biblical look at the topic of giving. I found myself eagerly turning the page to discover what God had for me to consider personally as a result of reading this book. I highly recommend it.

Todd Harper, President, Generous Giving

Jeff has captured such a unique view of giving to God in Plastic Donuts, that I feel I have been cheated by not hearing this message sooner.

Pastor Rodney James, Sequoyah Hills Baptist Church

It is a rarity to read a book in which the author deals with the biblical principles accurately, the Pastor's concerns with sensitivity and understanding, and the reader's need for inspiration and application.

Pastor Paul Taylor, Liberty Church

Prior to hearing the "acceptable gift" message, our knowledge of Christian giving was based on popular Christian culture. However, since hearing the biblical message, our giving has been transformed, manifested in joyful, mature, and more complete giving, to the Glory of God.

Andy and Wendy

Contents

*I am amply supplied, now that I have received from
Epaphroditus the gifts you sent.
They are a fragrant offering, an acceptable sacrifice,
pleasing to God.*

Philippians 4:18

Introduction

Plastic Donuts—They are everywhere, but frequently misunderstood. Few talk openly about them. When they do, it sometimes feels awkward or confusing, like something's missing.

Did you know the first murder in recorded history followed some hard feelings between two brothers about some Plastic Donuts?

We hear a lot of do's and don'ts about Plastic Donuts. The problem is, they often contradict each other. That's a real tragedy to me, because these Donuts can bring such joy and delight to the heart of God.

A man gave them after being stranded on an ark. God responded with a rainbow in the sky.

A man named Solomon gave some Donuts, and God visited him in a dream. Cornelius gave them and received a visit from an angel.

This is important stuff.

I'm Jeff Anderson, and this is my story about a Plastic Donut—a gift that was given to me. It really grabbed my attention, because I had been seeking to understand more about giving for many years. That gift opened my eyes to giving from God's perspective.

If you'll stick with me (it's a short book, right?), I trust you'll enjoy the experience, learn some things about God, and about yourself.

With all the different messages about the subject of giving, wouldn't it be great to get some clarity and peace about this issue?

When you see giving from God's perspective, the lights will turn on in your mind. You'll see that you really can feel good about your gifts.

My simple message about a Plastic Donut can change the way you approach this topic. Getting your mind and your heart on the same page is a beautiful thing.

Relax

I'm not a professional fund-raiser. This isn't a book about pressure or guilt. It's a book about the power of gifts, the way we give, and who we give to.

The Plastic Donut is about getting your own clearer picture of God as your Father and how He sees giving.

What you'll experience in this book can bring enormous freedom. You'll feel the weight of uncertainty being lifted from your shoulders, and be challenged by what you see about your gifts. Some of the reasons we've been encouraged to "give" are weak, but some of the ways we've convinced ourselves *not* to give are also questionable. Fair enough?

A Plastic Donut helped me see giving, and God, in a new light.

Money Problems

I learned about tithing from my parents when I was a child, but I was twenty-five years old when I first heard about money taught in church. I recall hearing that we should spend less than we earn, avoid debt, and give 10 percent to the church. But there was a problem.

I had lived these principles since childhood. Still something was missing. I had a growing sense of financial peace in my life, but spiritual peace about giving was lacking.

Was there more to Christian stewardship than having a budget and a clean tithing record? It sparked a hunger in me to understand how God views giving and how my giving could actually get His attention.

We've all heard messages and statistics about the lack of giving. Yes, greed and materialism are real forces in our lives, but don't you think that deep down inside, Christians have a desire to give? I do.

Giving instincts are hardwired into us, but the mixed messages about the subject can be frustrating and cause us to tune them out. The appeals, demands, and "answers" will continue to bombard us.

That's where the Plastic Donut comes in.

1
The Plastic Donut

Autumn Joy toddled across the room and stood at the edge of my laptop-centered view. I was in task mode, typing away in my living room recliner. With Shirley Temple curls bouncing around her face, my eighteen-month-old daughter looked up at me. I looked at her. Then she handed me a Plastic Donut from her kitchen play set.

I looked at the Donut and back at her again. She was waiting for a response.

So I put the Donut up to my mouth and said with great animation, *"Yuuum, yuuum...thank you, Autumn! This is soooo goood."*

Then something beautiful happened. Her big brown eyes widened and her lips pushed a giant smile against her puffy cheeks. She stood up on her heels, shrugged her shoulders up to her ears, and let out a high-pitched squeal.

After soaking in the experience for a few seconds, she ran back to her kitchen and brought me a little pink spoon. Again, I responded, showing her my approval. This cycle continued a few more times as I began to collect plastic pieces from her kitchen set.

For Autumn, this gift exercise kept bringing her back to Daddy. For me, it kept me looking for my child's return. I was moved by the exchange. The interaction. The connection. I was so pleased.

The whole experience wasn't about the Donut (and believe me, I like donuts). If one of her older brothers had brought me a Plastic Donut, it wouldn't have been the same. Somehow the gift was exactly right coming from her, even if it was just a toy.

The AHA Moment

At that moment it occurred to me, this is how our giving must feel from God's perspective. Our gifts to Him are like Plastic Donuts.

God does not need our gifts or our money. But like a father moved by a gift from his child, our gifts can really get His attention.

For my daughter, the feedback from our interaction inspired continued giving. If I had not paid attention to her and expressed my delight, she would have stopped.

She was learning about the power of a pleasing gift, and learning about connecting with me as her father. Meanwhile, I was learning about God and how to better connect with Him as my Father.

For years, I had thought a lot about the receiver of my gifts: my church, my neighbor, my chosen charities. I had studied about the benefits to me as the giver, but I hadn't given much thought to my gift from God's viewpoint.

Could it be that I was experiencing some sense of what God experiences when I gave to Him?

And what about the thrill my daughter received when she saw the joy on my face?

I had never pictured the act of giving with such delightful reactions. Had I been missing opportunities to connect with God in deeper ways?

Suddenly, I saw giving from a different perspective.

Questions—Questions

We all want to give. We all like to give and receive gifts. We have a desire to honor God and would like to understand what God's Word says about giving. The problem is, our noisy culture has given many different "answers" to our questions.

I want to know the truth. I want some clarity and confidence in what I believe and how I live. How about you?

Here's a sampling of the questions we hear about giving:

What's the "right" amount?
Does the tithe still apply today?
Is the first 10 percent required, and everything else is a freewill offering?
What should be our motivation?
Isn't giving all about the heart anyway?

Have you ever played a new board game and didn't quite know the rules? It's awkward. You don't know when you're making the right moves. This is how giving feels for so many people.

There has to be some clarity in scripture that brings us a better feeling about giving – like the connection my daughter and I felt when I received that Plastic Donut.

Many Voices

After many years away from God, a young man rediscovers his faith. He visits a large church in his city. In a message on giving, the pastor rejects the concept of tithing. He says it doesn't apply today—just like animal sacrifices and other areas of the Old Testament law. Instead, this church supports something called "grace giving." Hungry to learn the "rules," the young man enjoys hearing something new.

A few weeks later, he visits another church in the area. They happen to be teaching a series on tithing and asking for commitments. The young man leaves this service asking himself, "What does the Bible really say about giving?"

Some leaders use New Testament teachings to prove the Old Testament no longer applies. Some use them to prove it still does.

Some encourage giving based on how prosperous you can become. Others encourage it based on how uncomfortable you can become.

No Bashing Allowed

Let's cut our church and ministry leaders some slack.

Pastors and teachers are not the only ones without consensus. Those with the questions are providing answers too. Often, these answers are more like thoughts and opinions. Blogs have "answers." So do participants in small groups and Sunday school.

You may have heard some troubling things said (and done) regarding financial offerings. But "the church" (preachers, televangelists, name your favorite target) is not corrupt. Neither are the vast majority of people in these positions.

We know it would be wrong to use the manipulation of a very few as an excuse to ignore *our* unresolved questions about giving. Remember, we're looking for personal clarity from scripture about something we desire to do.

Sometimes the *lack* of talk about giving is the problem.

Put yourself in your pastor's shoes for a minute. Can you imagine bringing up the subject of money from the pulpit? The best-intentioned leader (you're the pastor, remember?) would struggle with the challenge of teaching on this topic without appearing to have a conflict of interest.

The congregation expects the lights to work and the building to be clean. Just imagine wrestling with the need for expanded facilities or staff, all while faithfully supporting projects for missions and the poor.

Is it any wonder pastors are tempted to avoid deep discussion of the subject?

Churches and faith-based charities have a God-given passion for their particular cause. To them, their mission for the people they are called to reach is crucial. Bold appeals for monetary support are expected – and scriptural. Let's give our pastors and ministry leaders a break and consider that the disconnect about giving could be caused by *our* lack of clear, biblical perspective.

If you've received this book from your pastor or ministry leader, you know they want to bring light to the subject. Here's an opportunity to get on the same page and pray for all our eyes to be opened.

Expect Good Things

This book won't beat you up, bring guilt or confusion. Instead, you can expect to gain confidence and clarity.

I've had the benefit of learning about giving from various perspectives.

In my work with church and ministry leaders, I see how giving matters to their organizations. I've seen it even closer while serving on finance committees and among the elder board of my own church.

I've talked about giving with the homeless at a downtown mission shelter. They want to experience it too. And I've discussed these principles with the affluent while dining on steak and lobster. This subject weighs heavily on their minds.

I've talked with my grandfather about giving and have shared the same concepts with a class of fourth grade students.

This book is about cutting through the noise and "pat answers," while discovering truths that can be trusted and helpful for everyone. When your questions about giving can be answered with confidence, your connection with your Heavenly Father will grow stronger.

Money on My Mind

I cared a great deal about money as a kid. One Christmas, I received a small red safe to store my cash. A few years ago, I ran across this safe while helping my mom clean out her attic. I could still remember the combination: 30 on the left dial, 110 on the right!

Saving money was very gratifying to me. I often had things I wanted to buy, but would change my mind about the purchase because of a stronger desire to keep the cash.

I was a selfish kid too. Although not an excuse, this sometimes comes with the territory of being a saver. Savers like to accumulate. Spenders like to release. Both have to overcome their respective tendencies in order to give in ways that God designed.

As a child, I remember putting 10 percent of my earnings in the colored envelopes at church. I never thought about giving less than 10 percent. But I never thought about giving more either.

This created a tension in my heart, one that would play out in my mind for years. When the subject of giving comes up, a similar tension may arise in you.

I went to college and majored in accounting to keep close tabs on this thing called money. After graduating, I obtained my CPA license, but it wasn't long before I grew less interested in tracking other people's money and decided to go into business to make my own money.

Along the way, I continued to wrestle with this particular money matter: giving.

Things Are Looking Up

For a money counter who needed to know the price of every-thing, I especially wanted to know the price of this spiritual activity called giving. I had questions like, "How much should I give?" "Is there a biblical giving standard?"

When I first heard the "money" subject taught in church, I was sitting in a Sunday school class with my new bride. As we walked out of the church, she turned to me and said, "I believe someday you will be involved in a ministry like this." Neither of us knew how prophetic her words were. At the time, all I knew was that I couldn't get these thoughts about giving off my mind.

After my accounting career, I enjoyed a five-year career as a full-time stock trader. Some of my life's most powerful lessons were learned during this period. There were some dark days during my trading journey, mostly because I was accustomed to thinking like the crowd.

When I learned to think *against* the crowd, things changed for the better. When the crowd was buying, it was often time to sell. When the crowd was selling, it was often time to buy.

This against-the-grain thinking can be helpful to under-standing giving as well. After my Plastic Donut encounter with my daughter, my view about giving changed. I saw more clearly why the joy of giving can seem so elusive; it's hard to experi-ence it without looking up to the Father.

Often, instead of looking up with my gift, I was looking down. Instead of pondering God's reaction to my giving, I was occupied with my own. Instead of giving towards the One unseen, I'd been giving to what I could see.

The Donut experience gave me a fresh perspective that connected with my study of scripture and started to make sense. Along the way I found simple truth and simple answers to my questions.

Reset Button

Let's see how giving can be a part of our connection to God our Father. We all want our gifts to matter to Him, and we might even dare to believe that we can bring a smile to His face when we give.

So let's step out from the crowd and away from the noise. Let's reset our thinking and discover the answers to our questions...How does God respond to my gifts? Does God really care about them? Does He like some and dislike others? Let's find out together.

2
What Is Acceptable?

Everyone told me having a daughter would be different. After having three sons, I figured I knew what was coming, but I was wrong. Sure enough – it happened. My baby girl stole my heart. I was smitten by her. Years later, I still am.

In my own thoughts, I imagine God being enamored by His children. The young sons of Adam and Eve were surely adorable in His sight. We don't know much about the brothers, Cain and Abel, but surprisingly we know about their gifts. Like my Donut experience as a father, God enjoys receiving gifts.

Abel's Gift

When it was time for the harvest, Cain presented some of his crops as a gift to the Lord. Abel also brought a gift—the best of the firstborn lambs from his flock. The Lord accepted Abel and his gift, but he did not accept Cain and his gift... (Genesis 4:3-5 NLT).

It was a unique time in history for the earth's first two sons. Sin and imperfection were relatively new, and its destructive effect on what God had made "good" was well underway. Yet, I'm sure much of what God had made was still quite wonderful.

Resources were abundant. Needs were scarce. There were

no poor, no orphans, no sick or diseased. But there were gifts to God.

On one occasion, the brothers presented gifts from their profits. Interestingly, God viewed the gifts differently. One gift was viewed favorably, the other was not. The Hebrew meaning of the original text *(sha'ah)* suggests God regarded, respected, and gazed at Abel's gift in a special way.

Sibling rivalries go way back. God's preferential gift response exposed this one. Cain's feelings were hurt and he became angry.

You may know the rest of this sad story. Acting on his emotions, Cain took his brother out into the field...and killed him.

This is heavy drama to process so early in the Bible. Adam and Eve's fall and expulsion from the garden was enough to derail the "feel good" beginnings of the creation account. Now the first act of murder by one son against another is a downright crusher. What a scandal! Yet from God's perspective, a bright spot shines through it all – Abel's gift.

Several thousand years later, a God-inspired writer travels down memory lane. Abel receives the first mention among history's faith heroes. The description that would accompany his nameplate repeats that he gave a *more acceptable sacrifice* to God (Hebrews 11:4 ESV).

Still today, people are curious about Cain and Abel's gifts. For a story with so few details, theologians have many ideas. This much is clear: In the very beginning, God showed great interest in mankind's gifts to Him.

Like Plastic Donuts to a little girl's daddy, man's gifts to the heavens triggered reactions from God. But not all gifts were the same to Him. Not all gifts were acceptable.

"Acceptable"...A Pleasing Word

The English language doesn't have a word that fully expresses the idea of "acceptable." In today's dictionary, the word can sometimes mean "barely good enough." But in God's vocabulary, "acceptable" is a powerful concept.

David understood its meaning:

> *Let the words of my mouth and the meditation of my heart*
> *Be **acceptable** in Your sight,*
> *O LORD, my strength and my Redeemer.*
>
> (Psalm 19:14 NKJV)

Your Bible translation may say "acceptable," or it may say "pleasing." The words are often used interchangeably in scriptures.

Isaiah talks about the kind of fast that is **acceptable** to God (Isaiah 58:5). This would be a fast that is pleasing to Him, certainly not "barely good enough."

Paul instructs us to present our bodies *as a living sacrifice, holy, **acceptable** to God...* (Romans 12:1 NKJV). This would be a sacrifice pleasing to God.

When I think of "acceptable" in these ways, I imagine a word that could encapsulate the feeling I had when my daughter gave me that Plastic Donut.

What word could express a combination of delightful, surprising, perfect, tearful, proud, ecstatic, and happy?

That's what "acceptable" means.

In David's song to the Lord, perhaps what he was really saying was something like:

> "Let all that I say and all that I think about
> Bring a big, joyful smile to Your face, and make
> You really proud of me,"

Getting the picture?

Pleasing God…Really, It's Okay

Like any child who seeks to please his Father, Jesus was no different. He says, *For I always do what pleases him* (John 8:29). And we know God was pleased with Jesus. The Father said so Himself, with a voice that boomed from a cloud (Luke 9:35).

Even Moses, who enjoyed direct access to God, wanted to know that God was "pleased" with him (Exodus 33:13,16).

But when it comes to "pleasing God," bad doctrine often gets in the way. Some people view "pleasing God" like performance or appeasement in order to satisfy Him – or even enter heaven. Of course, this is wrong.

Others react negatively to "pleasing" because of their inability to please a parent, a boss, or a friend. This is unfortunate too. We may carry baggage from relationships on earth, but our relationship with God is different. It is pure. We can please God and for the right reasons. Our greatest aim in life should be to please Him, whether we are on earth…or in heaven (2 Corinthians 5:9).

The thought of pleasing God with our gifts should be very comforting to us. It felt good to Abel to please God with his gift, and it felt good to God too.

Part of our challenge with "acceptable" is that we see varying grades of acceptability. We see high, medium, low—or good, better, best.

But throughout scripture, we don't see multiple standards. God does not provide us with degrees of acceptability. It is either acceptable or it is not. And the acceptable standard is a very favorable one. Let's take a fresh look at these familiar stories about gifts.

Pleasing Aroma

Noah knew about God's interest in man's gifts. After the flood, he stumbled off the ark with his family and offered *some of all the clean animals and clean birds* as a sacrifice to God (Genesis 8:20). What a bonfire that must have been!

This had God's attention. He *smelled the pleasing aroma* and then made a covenant to never destroy the earth with water again (Genesis 8:21). The word *nichowach* (pleasing aroma) means soothing, quieting, tranquilizing. Like steaming hot coffee on a cool day, God has His sweet aroma moments too.

Man's sin nature could not be reversed (v. 21). Yet their gifts could still bring favorable reactions from God. In Noah's case, a smile of vibrant colors across the sky was a reminder of the pleasing relationship God desires with His children (Genesis 9:13).

If you want to know what launched the rainbow among the clouds, think of Noah's gift.

Eight hundred years later God formalized the gift-giving practices in new ways. Under the law of Moses, the Israelites presented "acceptable offerings" (Leviticus 1:3, 22:20). The animals for sacrifice were to be perfect. From the heavens above, God took in the pleasing aroma (Leviticus 1:9,13,17). And from the earth below, people took comfort in knowing God was touched by their gifts.

An Acceptable Lamb

Thanks be to God for his indescribable gift (2 Corinthians 9:15).

Fast forward another 1,500 years. During a certain Passover holiday week, "acceptable" lambs were being offered at the Jerusalem temple. Meanwhile, a most unique gift was being presented to God on a hillside nearby.

This gift was offered on a cross. This gift was God's very own Lamb. This gift was...Jesus.

Like the acceptable gifts in the past, He too was a *Lamb without blemish or defect* (1 Peter 1:19). And as hard to comprehend as it may seem to us, this gift was a *fragrant offering and sacrifice to God* (Ephesians 5:2).

Those who witnessed this "indescribable gift" quickly put the pieces together. Suddenly the history of sacrifices made sense. The gifts of the past were a picture of this gift—a completely acceptable gift.

Acceptable Gifts Today

A lot changed after that "indescribable gift." The animal sacrifices faded away, but acceptable gifts to God did not. God continues to find pleasure and fulfillment in our gifts.

The Apostle Paul describes the monetary gifts from the Philippians as a *fragrant offering, an **acceptable** sacrifice, pleasing to God* (Philippians 4:18). The Amplified Bible shows us the gifts from this perspective: *[They are the] fragrant odor of an offering and sacrifice which God welcomes and in which He delights.*

Our gifts today can do a lot of good. They can feed the hungry, heal the sick, encourage the brokenhearted, and spread the good news. But most importantly, they can please the God in heaven, connecting His children to Him.

Think about that. Wouldn't you like to know how your gifts can bring delight to your Father in heaven?

3
Does the Amount Matter?

With three young boys in our home, we are a family of jokesters and cutups. We like to have fun with each other. Our son, Gunnar, doesn't mind being the object of family jokes, and he sure doesn't mind initiating them either.

One day Gunnar came up to me with his hands behind his back and a goofy grin on his face. "Here you go, Dad," he said. He held out his hands and handed me…the Plastic Donut. Then he busted out laughing. I thought it was funny too. To show my approval, I wrapped him in a headlock and scrubbed his head with my knuckles.

After using the Donut illustration in our family talks and sermons, Gunnar figured out the Plastic Donut carried a special meaning for his dad's message. Even Gunnar understood that a plastic toy from a seven-year-old would not produce the same effect on me as it did from his younger sister. He knew that not all gifts are received the same way – even when the gifts are identical.

Many of us are playing jokes with our gifts to God. It may look like a few dollars in the plate, a small check here and there, or a sporadic string of checks that discontinue during the summer. For some, it might even be steady 10 percent giving. These gifts might have once been pleasing to God, but now that circumstances have changed, they're more like the donut toy from my seven-year-old.

You've heard it said before: "Every gift is special." "Every gift can make a difference." "No gift is too small."

For secular campaign fund-raising, this might be true, but there is a problem with such expressions. When it comes to our gifts to God, not all gifts are special. The Bible makes it clear that not all gifts are acceptable.

King David knew that a gift that cost him nothing was worth nothing to God. He was seeking out a location to offer a gift of burnt offerings. An attractive altar arrangement and team of oxen had been offered to David for free, but he insisted on paying for them at full market price (2 Samuel 24:22-25).

Acceptable gifts (ones that get God's attention) are amounts that matter. When the gift amount matters to us, it can matter to God too. When the amount doesn't matter to us, it doesn't matter to God. That Donut did not matter to Gunnar. It was not an acceptable gift from him.

Amounts that Matter to Us

We all have amounts that matter to us. They may be home mortgage payments, rent payments, car payments, vacation packages, furniture purchases, memberships, etc. Because these amounts matter to us, we are diligent to set aside the money for these items.

The question is, what are the amounts that matter to you? Do your gifts to God fit in this category? Are you as diligent in making these gift transactions to God as you are in making other financial decisions?

Close to Home

If you've ever borrowed money for a home, you know banks will loan money based on their projection of what you can "afford."

But those affordability calculations don't take into account other amounts, such as your gifts to God. If you want to give gift amounts that matter to you, then it's up to you to leave room in your budget.

When people purchase the maximum amount of what mortgage bankers and car financiers will loan, they commit a large portion of their incomes to these items. In effect, the amounts that matter will be decided *for* them.

The Amount Matters to the Heart

John is a twenty-six-year-old software engineer for a growing technology company. He's pretty satisfied with his $85,000 annual salary, and makes maximum contributions to his 401k.

He enjoys his $1,500 per month apartment near the mountains and his new mini-SUV. He is particularly glad he purchased the special edition sport package to haul his toys around. John is also excited about beginning his new life with Amy, his soon-to-be bride.

When she saw the velvet black box, it took her breath away. But when she opened the box, her reaction changed. She tried not to appear disappointed. When she found out John had purchased the ring for $250, she was devastated.

Amy was not a materialistic person. Yet she still found the gift to be deeply insulting. She sobbed, asking him if he really loved her.

John rose to the defense and said something that he would later regret: "The amount for the ring doesn't matter anyway. After all, it's the heart that counts."

In my discussions with Christians about giving, no opinion has been more frequent than this one: "The amount doesn't really matter…it's all about the heart."

I understand the good intentions behind this statement. The

problem is, the message is wrong. Often we use this "heart card" to avoid deeper questions about the amount we give. For some, this wrong thinking actually adds to the gnawing sense of guilt so many carry—but guilt should have no place in our life and in our giving.

While the heart is crucial in our gifts (we'll talk about that soon), the amount matters too. In fact, it's the *amount* that helps engage the heart.

During the famous message we call the Sermon on the Mount, Jesus taught the connection between our hearts and amounts. *For where your treasure is, there your heart will be also* (Matthew 6:21).

Wherever you invest your money, your heart follows. And if you spend an amount that matters, it will move a level of your heart that matters. The amount gets the attention of the heart.

Two Cars

I used to have two very different cars that sat in my driveway: an old car and a much newer, more expensive car. In the evenings after work I would take my boys outside to ride their bikes.

When they would ride into our driveway to make their turns, occasionally they would get their handlebars too close and bump up against the cars.

If they collided with my old car, I would run over to help them up and make sure *they* were okay. If they collided with my new car, I would run over to make sure my *car* was okay. Then I would scold the kids for being careless.

Why the difference in my reaction? Because the new car had more of my treasure, and therefore, more of my heart. The new car was worth more to me than the old car. The new car owned more of my heart.

Lifestyle

As a young adult, I was quite comfortable with a 10 percent gift amount. When my income was rising, the 10 percent was growing too. But the other 90 percent was growing faster. That's just the way the math works. So even though my 10 percent gifts were increasing in amount, the 90 percent was completely focused on feeding my lifestyle. For me, the 10 percent wasn't moving my heart like it had in the past.

If I wanted to go on a weekend trip, I would. If I wanted to buy a new gadget, I would. If I wanted to speculate on a stock tip from a friend, I would. Much of my time and attention was spent considering other things to do with the 90 percent. I spent very little time thinking about the 10 percent and zero time imagining a life of giving more than that.

I was diligent in giving an amount to God and would be welcomed as a faithful tither by today's church culture. But I was not giving an amount that really mattered to me. It was not an amount that influenced my lifestyle.

Unknowingly, my lifestyle froze my giving at the 10 percent level. When it came to my financial affairs, my lifestyle had all the influence.

The issue is not about me sacrificing my lifestyle. The issue is about me giving a gift that is connected to my heart. But because I have a tendency to attach myself to my possessions (remember my car story?), my giving needs to impact my lifestyle in order to get my heart's attention. And when my giving gets my heart's attention, it can get God's attention too.

The Heart of Worship

Singing a worship song is not necessarily worship, and neither is writing a check. But when the heart engages through a praise or hymn in a meaningful way, it becomes more than just a song.

And when the heart engages through a gift that matters, it becomes more than just a check.

What about you? Do your gifts engage your heart in worship? Do your gifts influence your lifestyle? Do your gift amounts matter to you?

From God's perspective, **the amount matters**.

4
Rule #1: There Are No Rules

Grandpa and Grandma were faithful church members. He served in church leadership, she sang in the choir. After Grandma died, I stepped in to help Grandpa with his financial bookkeeping. Each week he gave an amount to the church. At the end of each year he would ask me to calculate his various income sources so that he could round out the 10 percent tithe.

One day I asked Grandpa, "Have you ever thought of giving something different?"

"What do you mean?" he responded.

"Have you ever thought of giving more than 10 percent?"

I related giving stories to him—both biblical and personal—sharing what I had been discovering. As I spoke, something was happening inside of him. With a tear in his eye and a pen in his hand, Grandpa reached for his checkbook and wrote out a check to his church. It was a gift to God, and to the place where he had been blessed in so many ways. It was far beyond the amount he gave each month and even beyond what he gave each year.

I understood Grandpa's finances and I was sure of one thing about the gift. It was an amount that mattered to him.

For decades he brought the same gift to the altar each week —a tenth of his income. Never to my knowledge had Grandpa thought of giving more. His gift standard was locked in for life...almost.

But on that particular day, the ceiling on his gift standard was shattered, and he embraced a significant truth about giving from God's perspective:

When it comes to our gifts, **we determine the amount**.

Biblical "Standards"

There's plenty of debate about whether the Bible offers a giving standard. Many suggest the tithe is that standard. Others resist the idea of any biblical giving standard.

Interestingly, the quest for standards is not so pressing for prayer, fasting, Bible study, or church attendance. How about "honoring your mother and father"? It's a clear command, but who determines how we live that out?

From the Sermon on the Mount, Jesus provides instructions on giving, praying, and fasting. For each, He focuses on the heart standard, but does not expound on an amount standard (Matthew 6:1-18) .

We see specific examples in scripture: The widow gave all she had; Zacchaeus gave half; the Pharisees gave tenths.

David praised God seven times a day. Daniel prayed to God three times a day. Moses fasted twice for forty days from food and water. Daniel fasted twenty-one days from rich foods and wine. Where did these children of God get their standards?

They determined them.

It's human nature to seek biblical standards. *Just tell me what to do!*

What good thing must I do to get eternal life? the rich young man asked Jesus (Matthew 19:16; Mark 10:17).

How many times shall I forgive my brother? asked Peter (Matthew 18:21).

Let's be honest. Are we looking for a "rule" to follow so we can check it off our list? Or soothe a sense of guilt and confusion? It's always easier to follow rules than follow a living God.

The absence of rules can cause tension in determining the amount of our gifts. Abel likely dealt with this tension in determining his gift from the firstborn of his flock. Zacchaeus may have encountered this tension concerning his decision to give half of his possessions to the poor. God does not ease this struggle with a one-size-fits-all gift standard. This tension is healthy.

This tension exists because of our free will. This tension exists because God is not an IRS form. He is our Father who wants a relationship with us.

Think about a meaningful gift you have given for your most treasured relationships – perhaps a birthday gift, an anniversary gift, or a special occasion gift. Who determined the amount of these gifts? You did, right? The giver determines the gift. The same goes for gifts to God.

The Father's Day Tie

The problem with Grandpa's giving was not that he followed a giving standard. Standards are powerful tools that help us lock in healthy giving disciplines. Stephanie and I set personal giving standards, and we help our children set them too. Everyone should determine a personal giving standard in their budget.

And the problem wasn't the 10 percent standard. The 10 percent tithe served me well early in my journey. It is a solid amount for new givers and likely was for Grandpa early in his faith walk.

The problem with Grandpa's standard was that it was never really *his*. He saw it as the church's standard, the denomination's standard...and even God's standard. He was just a few years from his death before realizing the power and control he had over his gift decisions to God.

God is not looking for the same gift from all His children. He wants a personal gift.

A striped tie for Dad on Father's Day can surely bring him joy. But the exact same tie year after year can lose its appeal. And if we give it because we think that's what he's expecting, the gift is even less personal.

Don't let your gifts to God become this way. Remember, when we give, we should be looking up to God – not down.

Freewill Giving Is Not New

Years ago I learned of a church that decided they would no longer teach tithing as a giving principle. They replaced the tithe language with terms like "freewill giving" and "grace giving." Their explanation was that the 10 percent tithe was the Old Testament giving standard and no longer applied today—and that New Covenant giving is now governed by grace, not law.

I cringed when I heard this. It wasn't their position on tithing that had me stirred (a topic we'll look at later); it was their position on freewill giving as a "new" concept. Our freewill choice is as old as mankind. And freewill giving was the bedrock of the Old Testament giving system.

Most people think those living under the Old Covenant had everything spelled out for them. They just had rules to follow, like automatic tax deductions from a paycheck, right?

Nope.

Under the Mosaic law, God commanded the people to bring gifts to Him at the three annual festivals: *No one should appear before the Lord empty-handed* (Deuteronomy 16:16). But it was each person's responsibility to determine the overall amount *according to the blessings* they received from the Lord (v.17 NLT).

There were eight gift categories under the law. For half of

Gifts of the Old Testament Law

Category	Who Determined the Amount?	Burnt Animals	Non-Burnt Grain	Non-Burnt Animals	Land, Money, Other
Burnt, Peace Offerings	Giver	✓			
Sin, Guilt Offerings	Law	✓			
Vows, Freewill Gifts	Giver	✓	✓	✓	✓
Firstborn Gifts	Law	✓		✓	
Firstfruits	Giver		✓		
Temple Tax	Law				✓
Gifts to the Poor	Giver		✓	✓	✓
Tithes	Law		✓	✓	

For more research, go to AcceptableGift.org

these gifts, the amount was determined by the giver. The amount for the other gifts was determined by the law.

What most people today call "New Testament giving," or "freewill giving" was in full force under the law.

What was particularly delightful about the Donut exchange with my daughter, Autumn, was that I was not expecting it. I didn't ask her to bring me a Donut. It came from her own free will.

There's something about unsolicited gifts, determined by the giver, that makes them very pleasing to the recipient. It's the very essence of giving!

Freewill Commands—a Paradox

Just because God gives us the freedom to determine our gifts does not make any choice a pleasing one. To choose not to give freely and willingly is to ignore God's clear desires. This sounds paradoxical, doesn't it?

God commands us to give freely. These giving instructions come through scripture and personal promptings of the heart.

Direct Prompts

If anyone is poor among your fellow Israelites...be openhanded and freely lend them whatever they need...There will always be poor people in the land. Therefore I command you to be openhanded toward your fellow Israelites who are poor and needy in your land (Deuteronomy 15:7-8,11).

Then celebrate the Festival of Weeks to the LORD your God by giving a freewill offering in proportion to the blessings the LORD your God has given you (Deuteronomy 16:10).

Direct prompts are commands from God that direct our gifts. The Israelites were commanded to give freely and liberally to the poor. They were also instructed to bring freewill gifts to the festival. These commands seemed to carry the weight of the law.

In both cases, the prompts were firm and clear. Whether or not to give freewill gifts to the poor, or at the festival, was not an option. They used their free choice to determine the amount. Scriptures are filled with commands like these directing us to give freewill gifts.

Sometimes prompts are delivered straight to our hearts. Jesus delivered this kind of direct prompt command to Peter, Andrew, James, and John. He asked them to drop their fishing nets and follow Him. Levi received a similar direct prompt to leave behind his tax business. Jesus gave a direct prompt to the rich young ruler to sell everything he had and give the money to the poor. In each case, the commands were firm and clear.

Steve and Angie were sitting in church one Sunday when a funding campaign was being launched. A large gift amount flashed through Steve's mind. It was an amount that mattered to him – an amount far greater than any they had ever given. After church, Angie shared her thoughts about the campaign with Steve. He was shocked when she shared the same amount he had been thinking of just minutes earlier. They knew this was a prompt from the Lord, so they obeyed.

David was attending a ministry conference when a ministry leader asked him to prayerfully consider funding a particular project. Initially, David was surprised to receive such a request, especially for such a great amount. He shared the request with his wife and she was surprised as well. It was certainly an amount that mattered to them.

Shortly afterward, they learned of an unexpected revenue source they would soon receive. The amount, and the timing, matched up with the need they had been asked to pray about. They knew God was speaking to them, so they obeyed and committed the gift.

For both couples, God was directing prompts at their hearts. To them, the instructions were loud and clear. It was a call for obedience to give a freewill gift. In both cases, their connection to God grew stronger and their faith was strengthened. The experiences were beyond their giving standards, and actually produced a surprising sense of adventure and joy.

God may initiate direct prompts while reading His Word. He may nudge you through other people. It might happen at a concert, a baseball game, or while watching a movie with your family.

Whispers

Tell the Israelites to bring me an offering. You are to receive the offering for me from everyone whose heart prompts them to give (Exodus 25:2).

Like direct prompts, whisper prompts help us act on the command to give freewill gifts. These prompts are whispers from God. And while direct prompts often occur unexpectedly, whisper prompts are often heard when people are looking for them.

God used direct prompt commands to draw Stephanie and me out of our giving comfort zone. As we obeyed the prompts, we experienced new joys in giving and connected with God in fresh ways. Suddenly we found ourselves looking for further giving experiences. What we once considered comfort zone threats became appealing giving opportunities. And we began to recognize the whisper prompts more regularly.

Self Prompts

For I testify that they gave as much as they were able, and even beyond their ability. Entirely on their own, they urgently pleaded with us for the privilege of sharing in this service to the Lord's people (2 Corinthians 8:3-4).

There is another kind of prompt that comes with great enthusiasm. It's called the self prompt. The Macedonians were known for responding to these unique commands.

Despite their own impoverished conditions, the Macedonians gave wildly and generously to those poorer than themselves. It did not take an external prompt for the Macedonians to share their "little" with the poor in Jerusalem. They did so *entirely on their own*. This self-prompt behavior happens when people give themselves *first to the Lord* (v. 5).

Like Snowflakes

"Cringe alerts" can sound off when the topics of freewill gifts and commands are combined in the same sentence. This is partly because heart prompts are like snowflakes: No two heart prompts are exactly alike. Not everyone experiences them the same way.

I once experienced a heart prompt while listening to a man share his giving testimony. Meanwhile, a friend of mine who heard the same testimony found it to be offensive. His heart was not prompted at all.

On another occasion, I was listening to a giving message at a banquet. The message did nothing for me, but generated heart prompts for others at the table.

God initiates heart prompts to draw us near to Him. He knows what giving will do for us, and what it can do for Him.

When we notice a prompt, we should take it personally... because it is personal.

Heart Prompts Can Fade

So I thought it necessary to urge the brothers to visit you in advance and finish the arrangements for the generous gift you had promised. Then it will be ready as a generous gift, not as one grudgingly given (2 Corinthians 9:5).

One of the sobering truths about heart prompts is that they can fade.

Years ago a good friend of mine was going through a deep valley in his life. He was financially broke, facing serious legal challenges, and his family had deserted him. He was a dear friend to me, a "brother in need." God prompted my heart with the following:

If anyone has material possessions and sees a brother in need but has no pity on him, how can the love of God be in him? Dear children, let us not love with words or speech but with actions and in truth (1 John 3:17-18).

Stephanie and I talked about helping him with our material possessions. We were willing, and even discussed an amount that we might give. But I delayed. Eventually the prompt faded away, and we never gave the gift.

Paul found the Corinthian church in a similar situation. They had promised to make a freewill gift for those suffering famine-like conditions. But like me, they were slow on the follow-through. They delayed...and delayed some more. The initial prompts were fading fast.

Paul stepped in with some strong encouragement. It was a two-chapter nudge note, known as 2 Corinthians 8 and 9. It was loaded with prompts. Paul wanted their gift to be a generous one—an amount that mattered to them.

He even set up processes to help them follow through. In the end, he knew it was up to the giver to determine the amount. He told them, *Each of you should give what you have decided in your heart to give, not reluctantly or under compulsion, for God loves a cheerful giver* (2 Corinthians 9:7).

I have always regretted not acting on my earlier prompt. By God's grace, my friend has recovered miraculously, but I still feel a twinge when I remember the opportunity to bless that faded.

Freedom and Responsibility

The bottom line is this. **We determine** the amount of our gifts. There's God-given freedom in that – and responsibility too.

You may be sensing this new freedom as giving rules or limitations are lifted from your shoulders.

You may also be sensing more responsibility as you take greater ownership of a relationship with the Father.

Giving is not a "touchy feely" thing. It does not mean give only when you feel like it or wait until prompted. Action is involved and personal standards should be set. The **amount matters**.

As you move forward in relationship with God, you'll find these two forces, freedom and responsibility, working together in a very natural way.

5
A Two Percent Perspective

You may wonder when we're going to talk about tithing. This isn't your typical tithe message where the author takes a position for or against the subject using their favorite illustrations.

You won't hear anything about the tithe of Abraham, Jacob, Malachi, Melchizedek, or the Pharisees…or about blessings or curses, sowing seeds, or robbing God…or about the storehouse, the temple, the Levites, the law, the new covenant, or the floodgates of heaven.

You also won't hear ideas about how the tithe was for farmers, not fishermen; was applied to crops, not currency; was actually the last tenth, not the first; was expected two or three times annually, not just once.

But you will hear more about this: acceptable gifts. Remember, that's our theme.

As with other topics in this book, the tithe is an area where it really helps to step away from the crowd to see it biblically. Since there are crowds on both sides of the tithe debate, a fresh perspective may be in order for most of us.

Full Perspective

If you've spent any time studying giving statistics, you likely know about the 2 percent. That's the percentage of income people give, on average, to charitable or religious causes. I agree it's a disappointing stat—not the measurement, but what it means. It falls well short of the 10 percent standard that leaders often have in mind.

But there is a different 2 percent statistic that is more alarming to me, and is perhaps the reason for the first one. Of nearly 2,000 mentions of various gifts in the Bible (I know because I have counted them), just over 40 pertain to the tithe!

The mentions of tithing account for only 2 percent of the total gift references in the Bible. So in essence, a "tithe only" focus ignores 98 percent of God's guidance on giving. Perhaps today's 2 percent giving is the result of us working with an incomplete giving doctrine.

When we don't consider the wholeness of God's Word on a subject, like giving, things get messy. And because of this disconnect, the matter of the biblical tithe has split the "crowd."

Split Decision

A recent survey of the 100-member board of the National Association of Evangelicals showed that 58 percent do not believe the Bible *requires* tithing today while 42 percent believe it does.

"Required for what?" you ask. Good question. Required for salvation? Required to be in good standing with God? Required to be a good Christian?

The survey is not clear, but it really doesn't matter. Whenever I see surveys like these, however they are worded, the results are usually divided similarly.

For those who are wondering what the fuss is all about, the tithe means "tenth" and this first came to light in the Old Testament. Today tithing looks like giving 10 percent of one's income to the church. Not everyone agrees about how the practice of tithing should look today.

People Want to Know

When I speak to groups about giving, there is a consistent set of questions people ask. Most pertain to tithing.

Does the tithe still apply today?
Should we tithe on the gross or the net?
Must the tithe go to the church?
Should we tithe on inheritances?
Insurance settlements?
Home sale proceeds?
Tax refunds?
Plastic toys? (Okay, I made that one up!)

People want to know what the Bible says. I understand. I had the same questions too.

But as we continue together throughout this book, you're going to see that we can answer many of the common tithing questions if we understand the acceptable gift principles first. So hang in there with me.

What Did Jesus Say?

If anyone had a chance to clear the air on tithing, it would be Jesus. But He didn't do so.

Jesus mentions the tithe twice in scripture (Matthew 23:23; Luke 18:11-14). In both accounts He rebukes a tithe-abiding Pharisee for his respective heart condition. Like the rest of tithing references in scriptures, teachers are split on exactly what He means regarding its application today.

When He spoke to the disciples about giving, Jesus did not bring up the tithe. Instead, He says, *Give, and it will be given to you...For with the measure you use, it will be measured to you* (Luke 6:38).

When He spoke to the crowds, He said, *Store up for yourselves treasures in heaven...* (Matthew 6:20).

When the Pharisees asked Jesus about paying the Caesar tax, He responded, *So give back to Caesar what is Caesar's, and to God what is God's* (Matthew 22:21).

For those looking for tithe rules, His teaching clearly does not provide them. Perhaps this was purposeful. When it comes to questions like, "What measure should I use?" "How much treasure should I store up?" and "How much is God's?" the timeless principles apply:

The **amount matters**, and **we determine** the amount.

The Apostle Paul had a chance to clear the air on tithing as well. But he didn't. As author of nearly half of the New Testament books, Paul said much about giving, but he did not make a direct connection about how the tithe applies today. Neither did Peter, James, and John.

Church Giving—It's Clear

While the case for the tithe may not be biblically clear to everyone, the case for church giving should be. The matter of church giving is not exclusively tied to the tithe. Regardless of what one believes about tithing and its current day application, our responsibility to support the church is well grounded in scriptures.

When Jesus commissioned the first preachers for their travel assignments, He told them not to take any of their personal money or possessions. He instructed them instead to search for "some worthy person" who would support their needs (Matthew

10:9-11). Even before the early Church movement was launched in the book of Acts, the funding precedent was already set by Jesus.

The Apostle Paul used direct prompts commanding us to share materially with those who feed us spiritually (1 Corinthians 9:9-14). This includes gifts to support preachers, teachers, and directors of church affairs (1 Timothy 5:17-18). Like Jesus, Paul was clear about supporting church functions.

Mixed Signals?

There may be mixed reactions to this chapter. I expect that.

Some might be sensing a new freedom about determining the matter of the tithe. That's good. But remember, there is responsibility too. We're about to explore this more deeply.

Others may be unsettled by the idea that the tithe standard is not so clear. If so, you can relax.

We can all agree that standards are helpful. Still, more clarity is needed. How do **we determine** the amount to give to God? Is there another standard to help us?

That's what this next chapter is about.

6
Because I Can

Have you heard expressions like these? "If members of Christian churches gave at least 10 percent of their incomes, an additional $164 billion would be available per year for Kingdom work."

"If 10 million people chose to give $20 per week, the cost of five trips to Starbucks, $9.6 billion would be available."

Meanwhile someone has figured that $1 billion a year could fund the task of the "Great Commission."

How about the "Giving Pledge"? Bill Gates and Warren Buffett have called the world's wealthiest to pledge half of their net worth to charities over their lifetime.

I commend these good-hearted expressions. I would like to see all Christians giving at least 10 percent of their incomes. And I would like to see the world's wealthy give half of their possessions to the poor like Zacchaeus did.

And while these funding equations might seem to resolve the world's inequities, God does not express His economy in these ways.

God's financial model for solving the world's inequities is for everyone to give **according to their abilities**. It's a simple plan.

Ability Giving—An Acceptable Standard

*The gift is **acceptable** according to what one has, not according to what he does not have* (2 Corinthians 8:12).

Before he was named Paul, Saul was the strictest of Pharisees, following all of the known religious rules. Whatever commitment to tithing he once held, we have no record of instruction about it in Paul's letters. But he was clear about a particular giving standard – the ability standard.

As the needs of the famine-stricken Judeans morphed to crisis levels, Paul desired the Corinthians to give a special kind of gift – an acceptable gift.

This acceptable kind of gift was based on their *means* (2 Corinthians 8:11), or in other words, their abilities.

Remember the self-prompting Macedonians? Paul says they gave *according to their ability, and beyond...!* (2 Corinthians 8:3 NASB). He wanted the Corinthians to apply the same standard for their gifts.

You may wonder where Paul found out about this ability standard. Consider these three sources:

Ability Giving—A Christian Standard

So for a whole year Barnabas and Saul met with the church and taught great numbers of people. The disciples were called Christians first at Antioch (Acts 11:26).

After a season of persecuting Christ-followers, Saul had a conversion experience of his own. During his new ministry training, he witnessed one of the most striking characteristics of these folks called "Christians."

Around that time a prophet named Agabus prophesied that a severe famine would cover the entire Roman Empire. That must have been a prompt to these "little Christs." Notice how they responded:

So the disciples determined, everyone according to his ability, to send relief to the brothers living in Judea. And they did so, sending it to the elders by the hand of Barnabas and Saul (Acts 11:29-30 ESV).

Just years earlier, Saul was on the scenes to officially witness the ugly persecution of these believers. Now this same man is on the scene to witness these acceptable gifts to the poor—gifts from the very men he once set out to kill.

Based on earliest biblical definitions, Christians are those who give according to their abilities.

Ability Giving—Christ's Standard

I tell you the truth, this poor widow has put more into the treasury than all the others. They all gave out of their wealth; but she, out of her poverty, put in everything – all she had to live on (Mark 12:43-44).

I'm sure Paul heard about the account of the widow who gave *two very small copper coins, worth only a fraction of a penny* (Mark 12:42). Jesus compared her gifts against that of the rich. Even though she was poor, the widow had a benchmark for a superior gift – it was her ability.

The story about the rich fool would have influenced Paul's convictions about giving also. Jesus rebuked the farmer because he stored up his wealth for himself but was *not rich toward God* (Luke 12:21).

Jesus did not say the farmer was not a giver. He may have even been a lawful tither. All we know is that he was not rich toward God. This "rich toward God" standard is connected to our ability.

Ability Standard—An Old Testament Standard

Paul would have adopted the ability standard from what he knew about the law as well.

Like the principle of **we determine**, the principle of **ability** is not only a New Testament concept. God has been measuring gifts based on ability for a long time.

For freewill offerings as part of the tabernacle building campaign, the Israelites were told, *From what you have, take an offering for the Lord...* (Exodus 35:5).

David understood this standard and told God, *Now with all my ability I have provided for the house of my God the gold... silver...bronze...iron...wood...onyx stones...* (1 Chronicles 29:2 NASB).

As part of the temple rebuilding campaign many years later, the people gave freewill offerings to the temple treasury *according to their ability...* (Ezra 2:69).

In reference to the three holiday festivals, the people were commanded: *No man should appear before the Lord empty-handed: Each of you must bring a gift in proportion to the way the Lord your God has blessed you* (Deuteronomy 16:16-17).

In the case of the burnt offering, the Israelite was to offer this voluntary gift according to his possessions. If he owned a herd, then he would offer a bull, but if he did not have a herd but a flock instead, then a burnt offering of a sheep or a goat would be acceptable. If the Israelite did not have a herd or a flock, then the offering could be a turtledove or a pigeon. The burnt offering accepted was based on the means, or ability, of the Israelite.

A Pigeon for a Lamb

After Jesus was born, Mary took Him to the temple to be con-secrated to the Lord. She offered a sacrifice in keeping with the law, *a pair of doves or two young pigeons* (Luke 2:24).

This suggests Mary could not afford a lamb of her own. According to the law, she could offer two birds—one as a sin offering for the ceremonial purification; and the other as a voluntary burnt offering in place of a lamb (Leviticus 12:8). Mary gave gifts based on her ability.

It is ironic that for a mother who had no lamb to give, God would give her His Lamb instead. She would raise Him and love Him as her very own. Thirty-three years later this Lamb would give of His complete ability, His life and blood, as the acceptable gift for the sins of the world.

This Lamb was a gift to God, and a gift for us. When we give according to our ability, we honor the One who gave all of His ability.

Ability Giving—What Does it Look Like Today?

After Stephanie and I married and merged our finances, we began to give jointly. The only standard either of us had known was the 10 percent tithe. After that Sunday school experience I shared earlier, we began to ask the famous question—should we give 10 percent of our gross income or net income?

When you approach these questions with an open heart, God's promptings begin to work. This process is not without some tension. For us, the decision to give more would involve trade-offs with other amounts that mattered to us. But as we found ourselves looking up with our gifts—these amounts began to matter too. Ultimately, we determined to give the greater amount for one simple reason: because we could. We had the ability.

Then new questions surfaced. Are we to give just 10 percent? Should we give 11 percent or 20 percent? What is the biblical standard? I continued to flip the pages in my Bible looking for the rules on giving. I didn't find the chapter with the rules, but we discovered plenty of prompts.

Like before, these decisions involved more trade-offs. But

the more we considered the prompts, the more clearly we saw God's blessings in our lives—salvation, family, peace, contentment, provision, etc. Somehow this perspective caused us to view our abilities more plainly and our limitations less so. Instead of asking "why," we began to ask "why not?" Giving decisions became easier.

With each step in the journey came a deeper connection with God. Sometimes we experienced His touch through direct financial blessings. At other times we didn't notice anything material—but rather a peace that surpasses all understanding—a smile from God taking pleasure in our gifts.

Profit, Possession, and Paid-for Abilities

A friend of mine made a commitment to give towards a church capital campaign. His three-year pledge was based on an expected sales commission stream from a new product. Three years later, the product never materialized. Neither did the anticipated income. He was not able to meet his pledge from his profit (income) ability.

After prayer, reflection, and sensitivity to prompts, he recognized he could still give the gift based on his possession (asset) ability. He knew his prized boat possession was worth the amount of the commitment. So he sold the boat that had served his family and friends for many years and he gave his gift to God. My friend discovered the truth himself: giving more because you can.

This also represented the heart shift that we've seen in so many people: Instead of finding reasons not to give, he looked for ways to be a joyful giver.

There is another ability we may have. I call it "paid-for" ability. Suppose your son or daughter receives a college scholarship. The money you may have set aside for this purpose is now available to you again, increasing your ability. Maybe your employer has provided you a company car or car allowance. This stretches your personal budget dollars, increasing your giving ability. Maybe your employer provides you a cell phone. Again, this increases your ability. Maybe your friend unexpectedly buys your lunch. You now have an unexpected ability to give.

You may not think you have the ability to give. But if you pay attention, you'll be surprised just what abilities you really do have.

Lifestyle Choices

Tapping your true giving ability will require counter cultural lifestyle choices—like debt-free living or reduced lifestyle spending. Unfortunately, many have forfeited their giving ability due to poor financial choices. Just a few unplanned moves can tie up your giving ability. But a few planned moves can free them up too.

Years ago Stephanie and I made the commitment to become completely debt-free so we could direct the savings towards our giving lifestyle. We made sacrifices to reach our goals. Now, without house or car payments, we have been able to commit more of our ability towards gifts to God.

We have had the privilege of attending celebrations for families who have reached debt-free milestones. Instead of using their new freedom to upgrade their lifestyles, they are tapping their regained abilities for gifts to God. We also know families who have downsized in order to restore giving ability to their financial lives.

Faith Abilities

When you have a relationship with the living God, heart prompts will test your faith abilities, not just the financial ones.

God may initiate heart prompts to give an amount that matters in a big way. You might not think you can afford the gift. Or maybe you can afford it, but you're not sure how it will affect your retirement, next summer's vacation, or maybe even next week's utility bill.

The self-prompting Macedonians did not have much financial ability to give from their impoverished conditions. But their faith ability carried them through in giving a powerful gift.

We learn in Hebrews that *without faith it is impossible to please God...* (Hebrews 11:6). Since acceptable gifts are gifts that please God, it reasons that our giving should involve faith. God grows our faith to deepen our walk with Him.

Back to Tithing

When heart prompts sound off, financial abilities start talking and faith abilities begin stretching, the "we determine" sensors go to work – and giving decisions start to flow.

Next thing you know, the technical questions about matters like tithing go away. Questions about giving off the "gross or the net" go with it. The question of whether or not to tithe from a tax refund, inheritance, and other abilities may change to considering whether to give a third, or a half, or even all of it as a gift to God.

You still may not be able to articulate a theological position on the biblical tithe and how it should apply in every situation. But it won't really matter – you'll find your gifts being guided by ability and the satisfaction of giving acceptable gifts.

But What If I Can't

Perhaps you are in a rotten financial situation, and from your view there's no way you can give. It could be due to a burdensome debt load, a marriage crisis, extended unemployment, or all of the above.

The story of the New Testament widow shows that most of us always have something to give. Elijah instructed an Old Testament widow to give her very last meal. Even as she and her son were about to die of hunger, she learned she still had an ability to give (1 Kings 17:10-15).

There may be times when you need to take ownership of poor financial decisions and even seek forgiveness. You might have to make some gut-wrenching decisions; like selling your home, forgoing a vacation, or canceling satellite television. I have a friend who went a full year without eating out—even for cheap, fast food – in order to reduce his debt.

As you take these steps, making room for gifts to God, He will surely notice. You might not be able to give much, and your faith ability might be running low too. But rest assured that your gift can still reach God. No matter what your ability or inability, God can be pleased with your gift.

Coming to Peace with the Tensions

I don't believe the questions ever go away completely. Perhaps you have some new ones. ("Thanks a lot, Jeff!")

How simply should I live? How much debt is too much? How much home is too much? How much vacation is too extravagant? How much savings do I really need? How much faith do my gifts involve? If you experience these tensions, that's good. I have them too.

But by now, we have clear scriptural guidelines for these types of questions. When it comes to our gifts, we know **the amount matters**. And when selecting our gifts, **we determine the amount**, in order to delight our Father.

In measuring whether our gift is the "acceptable" kind of gift, God measures it **according to our ability.** He understands our ability and takes it into consideration, not as a bill collector, but as a loving Father.

There will always be a healthy tension within us as we live the Christian life. At the same time, there is a growing peace deep within that comes through a connection to God—a connection that deepens with giving acceptable gifts to Him.

7
All the Difference

The sanctuary was at full capacity on "Harvest Sunday." It was the final day for celebrating the capital campaign and for bringing the gift commitments to the altar.

Chuck stood with his wife, Ellen, in the row directly behind the pastor. Ellen noticed Chuck was restless throughout the service, but she didn't think anything of it. As the campaign chairman, Chuck extended several public appeals throughout the month, and conducted a series of vision-casting sessions in homes.

They were emotionally invested in the campaign and had committed a significant gift that they were looking forward to presenting. At the appropriate time, the pastor stepped up to the pulpit to invite the congregation to bring their gifts. After a heartfelt prayer, the music began and Chuck quickly stepped out into the aisle with Ellen. He knew his quick action would serve as a cue for the rest of the congregation to follow.

Chuck and Ellen knelt together at the altar for a silent prayer. The crowds began to surround the platform. Chuck and Ellen stood up and walked by the decorated treasure chest. Chuck dropped the envelope into the box. As they returned to their seats, Chuck's palms were sweaty. While his right hand wrapped around Ellen's waist, his left fist was clenched inside his pocket. And inside that fist was the check.

Little did Ellen know, the envelope they dropped in the chest was empty.

When the service was over, Chuck gathered his family and left as quickly as he could. He wasn't even interested in hanging around for the team to tally up the offering. After a hurried lunch at home with the family, Chuck left for his office. He told Ellen he had something to take care of.

Sitting in his office after tense moments of hesitation, he finally pulled out his phone and made the call. It was a call he had thought about for years, but a mixture of fear and pride always stepped in the way.

"James, this is Chuck."

It had been four years since they had seen each other. It had been even longer since they talked cordially without attorneys in the room. Despite the lapse, no introduction was necessary.

"James, I want you to know I really regret what happened. I know there's much water under the bridge and that we failed to resolve things out of court. I am truly sorry for my part in it all. I hope you will forgive me."

The conversation was short.

Chuck knew they would never be best friends again. They wouldn't play golf or attend civic dinners with their spouses together. Yet something significant took place from that phone call. A burden had been lifted from his heart.

As Chuck hung up the phone, he leaned back in his chair and sighed. Then he stood up and reached in his pocket. He felt the check. Of course he knew it was still there. Immediately he left the office and called Ellen to explain the situation. On the way home, he stopped by the church and went inside to leave their check.

The gift was now complete—and acceptable.

Don't Leave Home Without It

Therefore, if you are offering your gift at the altar and there remember that your brother has something against you, leave your gift there in front of the altar. First go and be reconciled to your brother; then come and offer your gift (Matthew 5:23-24).

May I ask you to read Jesus' giving instructions again? It's important. What would you say that He is more concerned about: the money? Or maybe something else?

We often hear, "It's all about the heart." I just wonder if we really know what that means. When my dad first taught me about communion, I realized it was my chance to clean my conscience. It was a way of seeing the priority God places on the condition of my heart.

Ananias and Sapphira learned this heart lesson the hard way. They gave a special gift but lacked the proper heart to go with it. They lied to God about their gift. What started as a freewill gift expression ended with a tragic family funeral (Acts 5:1-10).

When it comes to our gifts, we know the **amount matters**. We know that **we determine** the amount, and we know God measures the gift **based on our ability**.

In the end, it is the condition of the **heart** that makes the gift pleasing to God.

The Heart vs. the Gift

*To do what is right and just is **more acceptable** to the Lord than sacrifice* (Proverbs 21:3).

Does the Lord delight in burnt offerings and sacrifices as much as in obeying the Lord? To obey is better than sacrifice, and to heed is better than the fat of rams (1 Samuel 15:22).

God desired the hearts of the Israelites over the blood of animals. And today He desires the hearts of His children over their gifts of money and possessions. Even Jesus acknowledged that it wasn't His body that God desired – it was His submission to God's will (Hebrews 10:5-7).

Remember, our money is like Plastic Donuts to Him.

This is where it gets tricky. On one hand, God doesn't want our gifts without our hearts being clear. On the other hand, we learned our heart isn't fully expressing love (for God or others) without gifts.

Just because one is desired more than the other does not mean one is not desired. Without a heart that pleases God, our gifts have limited value. And without gifts that please God, our heart expression is limited too.

Not Either

I'd prefer my little girl's heart over a Plastic Donut any day. But I sure enjoy having both. And how could I see that I had my little girl's heart if it weren't for her actions? And that is the case with God. And that is why He designed us that way.

As we learned earlier, our hearts and our stuff are connected. And therefore, one way we speak from our heart is through our gifts.

Paul instructed the Corinthians to prove their love by their gifts (2 Corinthians 8:8,24). James says religion that God accepts as pure is to look after widows and orphans (James 1:27). John says that to not share your material possessions with those in need is to not have the love of God in your heart (1 John 3:17).

On the flip side, Paul warns the Corinthians that if one gives all they have to the poor but has not love, the gift is worthless (1 Corinthians 13:3). And while the Pharisees were proud of their faithful tithing record, Jesus rebuked them for neglecting the *more important matters of the law—justice, mercy and faithfulness.* He did not let them off the hook for their gifts. Instead, He admonished them to right their hearts, while continuing their giving (Matthew 23:23).

The gift helps the heart speak what it really feels. And the heart makes the gift count for what it's really worth. The gift and the heart—they work together.

Christian Philanthropy

Could it be that a giving lifestyle apart from love and obedience to God is simply philanthropy? Jesus says, *No branch can bear fruit by itself* (John 15:4). A giver who does his work apart from the vine – Jesus – is *like a branch that is thrown away and withers* (v. 6).

If you have been operating as a "Christian Philanthropist," perhaps you're seeing how giving with a realigned heart can deepen your walk with God. You can relate to the Father in a new way.

Give to Get

Whoever sows sparingly will also reap sparingly, and whoever sows generously will also reap generously (2 Corinthians 9:6).

When it comes to the matter of giving and the heart, people like to talk about motives. Perhaps the most popular one is the principle of sowing and reaping. People have strong opinions about it. For some, sowing and reaping is a primary motive for giving. Others consider it an inferior motive, the bottom rung on the ladder of spiritual maturity.

So how does God view sowing and reaping as a giving motivation?

Give to Get Works for Papa

"Papa," my dad, loves his eight grandchildren, and Papa knows his grandchildren love sweets. When he comes out with a package of cookies or a box of popsicles, the little ones start heading in his direction. They crawl to his ankles, up into his lap, and say, "Papa, Papa."

He knows he is appealing to their desires, but he's okay with that. He understands the mind of a child. In fact, if you ask the younger ones why they like going to Papa's house, they might say, "He gives us treats." This is Papa's system. He likes the attention, and the kids like the sweets.

In the process, the rewarding techniques draw the grandchildren closer to Papa – into his arms, his love, and his presence. With time, the attraction to Papa matures beyond the desire for treats.

The children begin to learn his voice, his laugh, his love, his character, and the comfort and security they find in his presence. Their love for Papa becomes more pure. You can see it in their eyes and when they embrace his neck. You can hear it in their voice when they say, "I love you, Papa."

We are God's children, and we should take pleasure in God's rewarding ways, not reject or debate them. If one of the grandchildren would reject Papa's reward, it would dampen his spirit. God wants to reward His children for behavior that pleases Him – behavior that leads towards a connection to God with greater peace, joy, security, trust, dependence, gratitude, worship, and love.

Rewarding Motivations—That's God's Job!

There is something else meaningless that occurs on earth: the righteous who get what the wicked deserve, and the wicked who get what the righteous deserve... (Ecclesiastes 8:14).

When it comes to the principle of "sowing and reaping," not everything shakes out here on earth like we think it should. Solomon found it perplexing that the righteous may suffer while the wicked may prosper. But he understood God's judgment is not finished until later (Ecclesiastes 12:14).

Often, when we give, we experience financial blessings. Sometimes the blessings may come in less tangible forms, or in ways we won't fully experience until eternity. If rewards were predictable, giving would not involve faith.

When we do reap a miraculous return from heaven, it is natural to become excited. When our hearts are aligned properly, we will see that something bigger is happening. God is getting our attention.

Remember when Peter experienced a net full of fish in response to obedience to Jesus? (John 21:6). More important than the fish, Peter experienced the miracle provision of God. Immediately Peter jumped out of the boat, abandoned the fish, and ran to Jesus. Like Papa with a box of treats, God uses miracle blessings to send us running into His arms as well.

Another reason God blesses us is so that we will continue to give from our increasing abilities: *You will be enriched in every way so that you can be generous on every occasion...* (2 Corinthians 9:11).

God is the One who measures our motives. He knows the condition of our hearts and therefore the purity of the gift. We do not need to rank spiritual motivations for each other...and certainly not for God.

Back to the Heart of the Matter

As a father to four children, I've learned a lot about parenting. And I still have much more to learn. One of my discoveries is how enjoyable life is for me when my kids have their hearts lined up right – and how painful it is for me when they do not.

But no matter how far they stray, it's easy for them to get back into my fellowship.

Getting to the point of repentance may be difficult, but that's their part. Receiving my forgiveness is instant. When it happens with my children, the breakthrough is powerful. Immediately we're off to a fresh start. Like the prodigal son who drifted from his father, his return was welcomed instantly and completely.

Perhaps you started reading this book about giving, but now this chapter has you thinking of something else. Perhaps your heart condition is standing in the way of giving an acceptable gift. It might be a sin problem. It might be an attitude problem. It might be unconfessed wrongs. It might be a strained relationship.

No matter what it is, you are just a few easy steps away from a heart reset and restored fellowship with God. You may already be on a giving journey, but now you want it to count in new ways. This is your chance to right your heart with God.

Start by looking up, not at your bank statement or your bills or your problems or your past. Look up. Give your heart and soul to God. Then sense His smile. Sense His pleasure in you. Feel His embrace.

Now imagine Him receiving your gift. Like a Plastic Donut in a daddy's hand, imagine the gift falling to heaven's floor as God picks you up in His arms and assures you that what He really desires is your heart...and that the Donut is just a tool for you to give it.

Get that picture?

8
That Chair

In my living room is a big cream-colored leather chair that belonged to Grandpa. I am very comfortable in this chair. It's where I sit while reading my Bible in the mornings. It's where I sit when I address the family for family time. It's the very chair I sat in when my Autumn Joy approached me with the Plastic Donut. It's a great chair.

God has a chair like this too. A man named John caught a glimpse of it while receiving a most unique vision. His vision is known as the "Revelation of Jesus Christ." In the vision, an angel shared many scenes from heaven. Among them was one of the most breathtaking gift accounts ever described, and it took place at "that chair."

In John's vision, "someone" is sitting at a chair, or throne, in heaven (Revelation 4:2). Encircling the throne is a rainbow (v. 3). (It is interesting how these rainbows seem to appear at the scene of gifts to God. Remember Noah's gift?)

Surrounding the throne is a host of elders. Each elder is dressed in white, wearing a crown of gold on their head and sitting on their own chair (v. 4). The elders are falling down and casting their crowns before the throne.

These crowns were special Donuts—acceptable gifts for sure. Certainly the gold crowns were **amounts that mattered** to the elders. That is why they gave them.

I suspect the elders each **determined,** freely and willingly, to give their crowns as a natural response to worship. Group-think behavior has no place when standing before that chair.

Each elder gave **according to their abilities**—from the crowns on their heads. Ironically, these crowns were likely the rewards they received for how they stewarded their previous abilities.

And the **heart**? Well, check this out. As the elders fell before the throne, they cried out,

> *Worthy are you, our Lord and God,*
> *to receive glory and honor and power,*
> *for you created all things,*
> *and by your will they existed and were created...*
>
> (Revelation 4:11)

Often, when people refer to this gift scene, they talk as if it is a one-time event. Many assume we will all leave our crowns at the throne and walk away from them forever—sort of like the final scene of a play.

But closer reading of this passage suggests this gift scenario is being repeated over and over again (v. 9). Throughout eternity, we will bring gifts to that chair as we worship the King.

From John's Revelation we are told *the kings of the earth will bring their splendor into* the gates of the New Jerusalem (Revelation 21:24), heaven's capital city. There are twelve pearly gates to enter into the city (v. 21). Traffic will be busy for gift travelers.

This is great encouragement to us as God's children. God loves His children, and He loves to be worshipped by them. In heaven we will appear before His chair and present our gifts.

Until then, we continue to give gifts from afar; gifts of money and possessions that have been entrusted to us while on earth.

I hope you'll remember my story about the Donut, how our

gifts today can still reach the Father, even though we are not yet at His chair in heaven.

Online giving, wireless checks, bank drafts, giving kiosks—are just fine. Don't let them cheapen your gift experience. Our gifts can get the attention, touch the heart, and tap the delight of our Almighty God. Our gifts can travel!

So bring your gifts before Him. May they be pleasing and acceptable in His sight. And may your face light up as you imagine the joyful approval of your Father as He receives **you** in one arm... and your **Plastic Donuts** in the other.

He will sit as a refiner and purifier of silver;
he will purify the Levites and refine them like gold and silver.
Then the LORD will have men who will bring offerings
in righteousness, and the offerings
*of Judah and Jerusalem will be **acceptable** to the LORD,*
as in days gone by, as in former years.

Malachi 3:2-4

About Jeff

Since childhood Jeff Anderson has displayed a unique blend of financial behaviors: he was both conservative yet aggressive, cautious but a risk-taker.

As a trained accountant fresh out of college, Jeff admits he found himself daydreaming once about being a professional blackjack player. (Key word: "daydream")

That explains how after a five-year career as a CPA with a big-six accounting firm, he left to become a full time stock daytrader. For the next five years he spent his days staring at computer monitors, skipping bathroom breaks, and riding the roller coaster of market highs and lows.

Contrary to what his career shifts may suggest, there was something much deeper going on in his heart. For years Jeff reflected heavily on a basic spiritual matter—giving.

Through personal study of God's Word, his growing passion in this area led to another radical career shift. In 2003, Jeff joined Crown Financial Ministries, eventually serving as Vice President, North America - Generosity Initiatives.

Jeff continues to consult and speak with churches and non-profits. He is an elder in his home church, an active Bible teacher and financial mentor to many pastors and professionals.

Jeff is married to Stephanie and has four children: Austin, Cade, Gunnar and Autumn.

About Acceptable Gift

In 2003 I met a lady on the streets who was hungry and looking for food. After an unexpected shopping adventure together, I encouraged her to share some of her food with someone who had less than she did.

If there was ever a time I held God responsible for my words, that was one of them. That conversation and message weren't my usual order of business.

Later I came across a verse I had read many times: *the gift is acceptable according to what one has, not according to what one does not have (2 Corinthians 8:12).*

Suddenly this verse had new meaning to me. Whatever an "acceptable gift" is, everyone can give one - even the poor. Of course, I wondered what this might mean for me.

Through further study, I learned that an "acceptable gift" is the kind of gift that pleases God, gets His attention and connects us closer to Him.

What I discovered changed the way I thought about giving, and my connection to God as a Father.

We launched Acceptable Gift to present giving from God's perspective. With this biblical perspective, we help people find clarity for themselves, understanding the kind of gift that pleases God. Find yours at AcceptableGift.org

Jeff Anderson

I've known, and worked with, Jeff Anderson for nearly 10 years. He has lived his message which is solidly Biblical, and helps people see their giving in a new light. The Acceptable Gift brings leaders and those they serve, on the same page and connected to God in their generosity.

Howard Dayton, Founder, Compass-finances God's way

Ways to Chew
on Plastic Donuts

Have you been challenged and encouraged by these truths?

- **Share *Plastic Donuts* with your church**

   We have proven ideas and resources you can share with your church, including giving this book to each family, sermon notes, group studies, videos and more. Go to AcceptableGift.org for volume discout pricing.

   As families enter the lobby, they receive a copy of Plastic Donuts, and toy donuts! People were smiling. Being reminded that we are God's children is freeing, and exhilarating. People were also challenged. Seeing their gifts to God in a more personal way raised the bar for everyone. The subject of giving can be fun.

   Pastor Paul Taylor, Liberty Church

   Pastors and congregations are getting on the same page with giving, from God's perspective. See Acceptable-Gift.org for more information

- **Give *Plastic Donuts* as a gift to supporters of your non-profit ministry**

   This is a beautiful way to show appreciation, and help your constituents grow in their giving journey. Go to our web site and see video testimonials of people who have experienced giving from this fresh perspective.

- **Share *Plastic Donuts* with friends and family**

  Purchase a box of Donuts to pass along to those in your circle of influence. Help us spread these helpful biblical truths by sharing the message with others.

- **Check out our research**

  To learn more about the biblical research supporting the Acceptable Gift truths, go to AcceptableGift.org to sign up for insights and access to our free resources and blogs. Join the discussion!

- **The next time you give a gift, remember these truths**

  The amount matters.

  We determine the amount.

  We give according to our ability.

  The heart makes the gift count.

  Your gifts can delight the heart of God!

ACCEPTABLE gift
Giving from God's Perspective